Out and About at the Apple Orchard

Field Trips

Written by Diane Mayr • Illustrated by Anne McMullen

Content Advisor: Sam Nassar
Owner, Apple Acres Orchard, Windham, New Hampshire

Reading Advisor: Lauren A. Liang, M.A.
Literacy Education, University of Minnesota, Minneapolis, Minnesota

PICTURE WINDOW BOOKS
Minneapolis, Minnesota

Dedicated to Dr. Joseph R. Gordon—D.M.

Many thanks to Sam Nassar of Apple Acres in Windham, New Hampshire.

Designer: Melissa Voda
Page production: Picture Window Books
The illustrations in this book were rendered using watercolor and ink.

Picture Window Books
5115 Excelsior Boulevard
Suite 232
Minneapolis, MN 55416
1-877-845-8392
www.picturewindowbooks.com

Printed in the United States of America.
1 2 3 4 5 6 08 07 06 05 04 03

Library of Congress Cataloging-in-Publication Data
Mayr, Diane.
   Out and about at the apple orchard / written by Diane Mayr ; illustrated by Anne McMullen.
      p. cm.
   Summary: Describes all that is involved in growing apples—covering planting, pollination, harvesting, different varieties, and more.
   ISBN 1-4048-0036-0 (lib. bdg. : alk. paper)
   1. Apples—Juvenile literature. [1. Apples.] I. McMullen, Anne, ill. II. Title.
   SB363 .M39 2003
   634'.11—dc21
                                                                                          2002006283

We're going on a field trip to an apple orchard.
We can't wait!

Things to find out:
What does an apple farmer do every day?
Do you ever find bugs on the apples?
Do you use machines to pick the apples?
How do you make apple juice?

Welcome to Shiny Apple Farm. I'm Mrs. Pippin.
My husband and I own this orchard, and we'll be
showing you around. See all those lovely apples?
They're just waiting to be picked. Apple farms grow
many different kinds of apples. Some ripen in the
summer. Others ripen in the fall.

4

When apple trees are planted, space is left between the trees to move tractors and other equipment.

In springtime, apple trees grow flowers.
Honeybees visit the flowers. The bees carry
pollen from flower to flower and from tree to tree.
The pollen helps a flower change into fruit.

An apple blossom may be visited by bees 50 times, and one tree can have as many as 10,000 blossoms. Not every blossom turns into fruit.

7

Trees need food, water, and sunlight to grow. Early in the summer, we add compost to the soil to make the trees strong. Later in the summer, if there is not enough rain, we water the trees.

Compost is plant food made from grass and weed clippings, apple scraps, and other bits of plants. We prune, or cut out, the dead and broken branches a few times each year. This lets in more sunlight.

All summer we work to protect the orchard from pests and diseases. Pests are anything that harms the trees or apples, such as animals and insects. We sometimes spray apple trees with chemicals to stop disease and get rid of harmful insects, but we prefer not to use chemicals. We bring in helpful insects and hang insect traps and bars of soap in nets to help control pests.

Some apple tree pests are apple maggots, woolly apple aphids, and white apple leafhoppers. Some helpful insects are ladybugs and lacewings.

In late August, apples begin to ripen. From then on, we pick until late October. Now it's your turn to pick an apple. Put your hand around the apple and twist it. Tip the apple upside down. The stem should snap off the branch. Apples bruise easily. That's why we pick them by hand. Apples high in the trees have to be picked using ladders.

How do you know if an apple is ripe? Most apples ripen from green to red. Ripe apples should be firm, crisp, and juicy.

We check each apple after it has been picked.
We remove those that are bruised, hurt by pests,
or not the right shape. Some apples are packed into
bags for sale. The rest we put into cold storage.

Apples may be stored for up to six months.

15

We take the apples that are not the right shape and
press out the juice to make apple cider. We sell some
of our apples to other companies to make apple juice.

Both cider and juice are squeezed from apples, but they are not the same. Cider has tiny bits of apple in it and looks cloudy. Apple juice is clear.

17

We have 30 kinds of apples growing here, so there are
plenty of new apples for you to try each time you visit.
You can try lots of products made from apples, too.

We have applesauce, apple fritters, apple pie, and more.

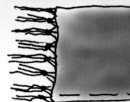

America's favorite apple is the Red Delicious. Other favorite apples are the Golden Delicious, Gala, Granny Smith, Fuji, and McIntosh.

Thanks for visiting us at Shiny Apple Farm.
I hope to see you all again.

FLOATING FRUIT EXPERIMENT

Have you ever bobbed for apples? If so, then you know that apples float. Apples float because they are 25% air. Do other fruits float? Let's find out.

What you need

an apple

several other fruits (suggestions: orange, kiwi, banana, grape, pear, strawberry)

a large container with at least 6 inches (15 centimeters) of water inside it

What you do

1. Float the apple. Is more of the apple above the water or below the water?

2. Hold another fruit in your hand. Is it larger or smaller than the apple? Lighter or heavier? Harder or softer? Is it the same shape? Do you think it will sink or float? Why?

3. Place the fruit in the water. What happens? Did you guess right? If it floats, is more of the fruit above or below the water? Does it float the same way as the apple? Do you think the fruit has more or less air than the apple?

4. Test the other fruits.

FUN FACTS

- A bushel of apples weighs about 42 pounds (16 kilograms) and contains about 100 3-inch (8-centimeter) apples.

- The apple blossom is the state flower of Arkansas and Michigan.

- October is National Apple Month.

- Each American eats about 46 pounds (17 kilograms) of apples a year. That's about 110 apples. Only 43 of the apples are eaten fresh. The other 67 are in apple juice and other apple products.

- The first apple is believed to have come from Kazakhstan, in Central Asia.

- China grows more apples than any other country. In the United States, Washington state grows the most apples.

- The first apples in the United States were brought over by ship from England. The first orchards were planted near Boston in the early 1600s. Apples were grown to make cider or to feed to farm animals, not for eating.

- Johnny Appleseed was born John Chapman in Massachusetts on September 26, 1774. During his lifetime, he walked more than 100,000 miles (160,900 kilometers) through Pennsylvania, Ohio, Kentucky, Illinois, and Indiana. He planted apple seeds wherever he traveled.

- There are about 7,500 of kinds of apples in the world.

- Pomology is the science of growing apples.

WORDS TO KNOW

blossom—a flower

bruise—to hurt without breaking the skin

bushel—a unit of measurement, or a container that holds a bushel of something

compost—a mixture of rotting plant matter that is used to feed plants

pollen—a yellow powder made by the male parts of a flower. The powder must join with the female parts of a flower before a fruit can form.

product—something that is made by people

prune—to cut weak, dead, or unwanted branches from a bush or tree

ripen—to become fully grown and ready to eat

TO LEARN MORE

At the Library

Burckhardt, Ann L. *Apples*. Mankato, Minn.: Bridgestone Books, 1996.

Gibbons, Gail. *Apples*. New York: Holiday House, 2000.

Landau, Elaine. *Apples*. New York: Children's Press, 1999.

Wallace, Nancy Elizabeth. *Apples, Apples, Apples*. Delray Beach, Fla.: Winslow Press, 2000.

Wellington, Monica. *Apple Farmer Annie*. New York: Dutton Children's Books, 2001.

On the Web

Washington State Apple Commission for Kids

http://www.bestapples.com

For fun orchard games and activities

County Line Orchard

http://www.countylineorchard.com

Learn about the kinds of apples grown at Indiana's County Line Orchard.

Want to learn more about the apple orchard? Visit FACT HOUND at *http://www.facthound.com*.

INDEX